THE CHRISTIAN'S SECRET OF A HAPPY LIFE

HANNAH WHITALL SMITH

BARBOUR
PUBLISHING

© 1996 by Barbour Publishing, Inc.

ISBN 1-55748-807-X

Cover image © PhotoDisc

Published by Barbour Publishing, Inc., P.O. Box 719, Uhrichsville, Ohio 44683, www.barbourbooks.com

Our mission is to publish and distribute inspirational products offering exceptional value and biblical encouragement to the masses.

ecpa Member of the
Evangelical Christian
Publishers Association

Printed in the United States of America.
5 4

PART 1:

THE LIFE

CHAPTER 1
IS IT SCRIPTURAL?

A keen observer once said, "You Christians seem to have a religion that makes you miserable. You are like a man with a headache. He does not want to get rid of his head, but it hurts him to keep it. You cannot expect outsiders to earnestly seek anything so uncomfortable." For the first time, I saw that Christianity ought to make its possessors happy, not miserable. I asked the Lord to show me the secret of a happy Christian life. I shall share this secret.

In moments of illumination, God's children feel that a life of rest and victory is their birthright. Remember your soul's triumph when you first met the Lord Jesus and glimpsed His mighty saving power? How easy it seemed to be more than conquerors through Him who loved you. Under the leadership of a Captain who had never been foiled in battle, how could you dream of defeat?

Many of you have found your real experience far different. Your victories have been few and fleeting, your defeats many and disastrous. You believe in Christ as your Savior from the penalty of sin but have not found Him as your inward-dwelling Savior from its power. Your early visions of triumph grow dim. You settle for the conviction that a Christian's life is alternately sinning and failure, repenting and victory, to be repeated again and again.

Is this all the Lord Jesus had in mind when He gave His life to deliver you from your cruel bondage to sin? Did His promise to deliver us from our enemies and enable us to triumph only mean sometimes? No! Jesus came to save you from the power and dominion of sin now, in this life. If you doubt this, search your Bible.

When the angel of the Lord appeared unto Joseph in a dream and announced the coming birth of the Savior, he said, "Thou shalt call His name Jesus, for He shall save His people from their sins."

Zacharias, "filled with the Holy Ghost," at the birth of his son, confirmed it through prophecy.

Paul and Peter insisted that Jesus' followers must walk a holy, Christlike walk, both for themselves and as an example to unbelievers. The fact that far more mention is made of present salvation from sin than of future salvation in heaven plainly shows God's estimate of their relative importance. Can we, even for a moment, suppose the holy God who hates sin in the sinner is willing to tolerate it in the Christian? Or that His plan of salvation does not include deliverance from the power of sin?

Dr. Chalmers says, "Sin is that scandal which must be rooted out from the great spiritual household over which the Divinity rejoices." Does not that same God who loved righteousness and hated iniquity six thousand years ago bear the same love to righteousness and hatred to iniquity still? The cross of Christ, by the same mighty, decisive stroke that moved the curse of sin away from us, also surely moves away the power and the love of it from over us." The redemption accomplished for us by our Lord Jesus Christ on the cross at Calvary is a redemption from the power of sin and guilt. Jesus is able to save to the uttermost all who come unto God by Him.

A Quaker divine of the seventeenth century said, "There is nothing so contrary to God as sin. It is inconsistent and disagreeable with true faith for people to be Christians and yet to believe that Christ, the eternal Son of God, to whom all power in heaven and earth is given, will suffer sin and the devil to have dominion over them.

"[Some] say you must abide in sin as long as you live. What! Must we never be delivered? Must this crooked heart and perverse will always remain? What sort of a Redeemer is this, or what benefit have I in this life, of my redemption?"

The story of freedom from sin and guilt through

the death of Christ has filled with songs of triumph the daily lives of many saints of God throughout all ages. It is now being sounded forth afresh to the unspeakable joy of weary and burdened souls.

Do not reject it, then, until you have prayerfully searched the Scriptures to see whether these things be so. Ask God to open the eyes of your understanding by His Spirit, that you may know "what is the exceeding greatness of His power to us who believe." When you catch faint glimpses of this power, learn to look away from your own weakness. Put your case into His hands; trust Him to deliver you.

CHAPTER 2
GOD'S SIDE AND MAN'S SIDE

Two teachers held meetings in the same place at alternate hours. One spoke only of God's part in the work of the life and walk of faith. The other dwelt exclusively on man's part. They were in perfect sympathy with each other and realized fully each taught different sides of the same great truth. One perplexed lady said, "I cannot understand it at all. Here are two preachers undertaking to teach just the same truth, and yet, to me, they seem flatly to contradict each other."

I give what I judge to be the two distinct sides to show how looking at one without the other creates wrong impressions and views of the truth.

In brief, man's part is to trust, God's part is to work. We are to be delivered from the power of sin and made perfect in every good work to do the will of the Lord.

Most of us try to do it for ourselves and fail. Then we discover the Lord Jesus Christ has come on purpose to do it for all who put themselves wholly into His hands. Plainly the believer can do nothing but trust. The Lord actually does the work entrusted to Him.

The preacher who is speaking on the man's part in the matter cannot speak of anything but surrender and trust. Such preachers are constantly criticized as though in saying this, they imply there was no other part. The cry goes out that the doctrine of faith does away with realities; that souls are just to trust and there is an end to it. This misapprehension arises when either the preacher fails to state or the hearer fails to hear the other side of the matter.

On the other hand, the preacher who dwells on God's part only is also criticized. He does not speak of trust, for the Lord's part is to bring to bear upon all the refining and purifying resources of His wisdom and His love. He causes us to grow in grace and conform to the image of Christ.

Sanctification is both a step of faith and a process of works. By a step of faith, we put ourselves into the hands of the Divine Potter; by a gradual process He makes us into a vessel unto His own honor.

How is a lump of clay made into a beautiful vessel? It lies passive in the potter's hands. It is not expected to do the potter's work, only to yield itself up to his working.

The potter takes the clay, kneads, and works it until it is pliable. Next he forms a vessel. He turns it, planes it, and smoothes it. He dries it in the sun, bakes it in the oven, and finally it is finished.

Once you have put yourself wholly and absolutely into the heavenly Potter's hands, you must expect Him to begin to work. His way of accomplishing that which you have entrusted to Him may be different from your way; but He knows, and you must be satisfied.

I knew a lady who entered into this life of faith with a great outpouring of the Spirit and a wonderful flood of light and joy. She supposed this was preparation for some great service and expected to be put forth immediately into the Lord's harvest-field. Instead, her husband lost all his money. She was shut up in her own house with no time or strength left for any gospel work. She accepted the discipline and yielded herself up as heartily to household chores as she would have done to preach, pray, or write for the Lord. Through this training, He made her into a vessel "meet for the Master's use and prepared unto every good work."

All we claim in this life of sanctification is that by an act of faith we put ourselves into the hands of the Lord then, by a continuous exercise of faith, keep ourselves there. When and while we do it, we are truly pleasing to God, although it may require years of training and discipline to mature us.

When we do our part, He does His. Do not be afraid. Trust is the beginning and the continuing foundation.

The apparent paradox of "Do nothing but trust" and "Do impossible things" can be likened to a saw in a carpenter's shop. We say, "The saw has sawn asunder a log"; then, "The carpenter has sawn it." The saw is the instrument used; the power that uses it is the carpenter's.

God's working depends on our cooperation. At a certain place our Lord could do no mighty work because of the people's unbelief. The most skillful potter cannot make a beautiful vessel out of a lump of clay never put into his hands. Neither can God make of me a vessel unto His honor unless I put myself into His hands.

As I am writing for human beings, I shall dwell mostly upon man's side in the hope of making plain how we are to fulfill our part of this great work. But I wish it to be distinctly understood: Unless I believed with all my heart in God's effectual working on His side, not one word of this book would ever have been written.

CHAPTER 3
THE LIFE DEFINED

The chief characteristics of living the Higher Christian Life, best described as the "life hid with Christ in God," are entire surrender to the Lord and perfect trust in Him. This results in victory over sin and inward rest of the soul.

Most Christians are like a man who toiled along the road, bending under a heavy burden. A wagon overtook him. The man joyfully accepted the driver's offer of a ride but when seated in the wagon continued to bend beneath the burden on his shoulders.

"Why do you not lay down your burden?" asked the kind-hearted driver.

"Oh!" replied the man. "It is almost too much to ask you to carry me. I could not think of letting you carry my burden, too." So Christians who have given themselves into the care and keeping of the

Lord Jesus still continue to bend beneath the weight of their burdens throughout the whole length of their journey.

By burdens, I mean everything that troubles us, spiritual or temporal.

First of all, the greatest burden, the most difficult thing we have to manage in life is self—daily living, feelings, special weaknesses and temptations that worry us and bring us into bondage and darkness. You must hand yourself and all you are over into the care and keeping of your God and leave it all there. Then rest, trusting yourself to Him, continually and absolutely.

Next lay off every other burden: health, reputation, Christian work, houses, children, business, and servants.

It is generally easier to commit our unknown future to the Lord than to commit the present. I knew a Christian lady whose temporal burden left her sleepless and with no appetite. One day she saw a tract, "Hannah's Faith," the story of a poor woman who had been carried triumphantly through a life of unusual sorrow. A kind visitor once exclaimed, "Oh, Hannah, I do not see how you could bear so much sorrow!"

Hannah replied, "The Lord bore it for me. When I take my burdens to Him, I leave them there. If worry comes back, I take it to Him again and again until at last I forget I have any worries and am at perfect rest."

You may be hungering for just such a life. You would be delighted to hand over your burdens and the management of your unmanageable self. Do you recollect the delicious sense of rest at the end of a hard, weary day? How delightful to relax every muscle, no longer to have to hold up an aching head or weary back. You trusted yourself to the bed and you rested.

Suppose you had dreaded each moment to find the bed giving way and landing you on the floor. Would not every muscle have been strained to hold yourself up and the weariness greater than if you had not gone to bed at all?

Learn to trust the Lord. Let your souls lie down upon the couch of His sweet will, sure He will hold you up. Your part is simply to rest. His part is to sustain you, and He cannot fail.

The Lord gave us an analogy: that of the child-life. For "Jesus called a little child unto Him. . .and said, 'Except ye be converted and become as little children, ye shall not enter into the kingdom of heaven.'"

A child lives by faith, its chief characteristic being freedom from care. Its life is one continuous trust in parents, teachers, sometimes even those who are unworthy of trust.

I once visited a wealthy home where there lived a little adopted child on whom was lavished all the love, tenderness, and care human hearts could bestow. I watched the child running in and out, free and lighthearted, a picture of our wonderful position as children in the house of our heavenly Father. How much more the great, loving heart of our God and Father must be grieved and wounded at seeing His children take so much care and thought!

Who is best cared for in the house? The little children. The least of all, the helpless baby, receives the largest share and is rejoiced in more tenderly than the hardest worker.

This life of faith is just this—being a child in the Father's house. Let the ways of childish confidence and freedom from care, which so please you and win your hearts in your own little ones, teach you what should be your ways with God. Leaving yourselves in His hands, learn to be literally "careful for nothing." You will find the peace of God which passeth all understanding shall keep your hearts and minds through Christ Jesus.

It is no speculative theory or dream of romance. There is such a thing as having one's soul kept in perfect peace, now, here in this life. Childlike trust in God is the key to its attainment.

CHAPTER 4
HOW TO ENTER IN

This blessed life is not an attainment, but an obtainment. The soul must fully recognize it is God's gift in Christ Jesus and cannot be gained by any efforts or works on our own. God can bestow the gift only upon the fully consecrated soul, to be received by faith and great thankfulness.

I once tried to explain consecration to the physician in charge of a large hospital. "Suppose in your rounds a patient entreats you to take his case under your special care in order to cure him but at the same time refuses to tell you his symptoms or take your prescribed remedies. He tells you, 'I am quite willing to follow the directions that seem good to me, but in other matters I prefer judging for myself and following my own directions.' What would you do?"

"Do!" the doctor replied indignantly. "I can do

nothing for a patient unless he puts his whole case into my care and obeys my directions. Doctors must be implicitly obeyed, if they are to have any chance to cure their patients."

"That is consecration," I continued. "God must have the whole case put into His hands, and His directions must be implicitly followed."

"I see it!" he exclaimed. "And I will do it; God shall have His own way with me from henceforth."

An entire surrender of spirit, soul, and body to His control in a life of inevitable obedience may look hard to a soul ignorant of God. To those who know Him, it is the happiest and most restful of lives. Could we but for one moment get a glimpse into the mighty depths of His love, our hearts would spring out to His will and embrace it as our richest treasure.

Some Christians seem to think all their Father in heaven wants to do is make them miserable. A Christian lady expressed how impossible she found it to say, "Thy will be done," and how afraid she would be to do it. She was the mother of an only little boy who was heir to a great fortune and the idol of her heart.

Her friend said, "Suppose your little Charley should run to you and tell you he has made up his mind to let you have your way with him; that he is always going to obey you and wants you to do what you think is best for him because he trusts your love. Would you say to yourself, 'Ah, now I shall have a chance to make Charley miserable. I will take away all his pleasures and compel him to do that which is impossible.' "

"You know I would not!" said the indignant mother. "I would hug and kiss him and fill his life with the sweetest and best."

"Are you more tender and loving than God?"

"Ah, no. I see now I must not be any more afraid of saying, 'Thy will be done' to my heavenly Father than I want my Charley to be of saying it to me."

Most Christians understand this principle when it comes to salvation but lose sight of it in living the Christian life. <u>Then</u> He was our Redeemer; <u>now</u> He is to be our Life.

Repeat these four words over and over with voice and soul, emphasizing each time a different word and let your faith lay hold of a new power in Christ.

<u>Jesus</u> saves me now—It is He.

Jesus <u>saves</u> me now—It is His work to save.

Jesus saves <u>me</u> now—I am the one to be saved.

Jesus saves me <u>now</u>—He is doing it every
      moment.

A lady now eminent in this life of trust once cried out, "You all say, 'Abandon yourself and trust.' I do not know how. Do it out loud so I may see."

Shall I do it out loud for you?

"Lord Jesus, I believe Thou art able and willing to deliver me. I believe Thou didst die to set me free not only in the future, but now and here. I believe Thou art stronger than sin. I am going to trust Thee to keep me. I have tried and failed. I give myself to Thee, body, soul, and spirit. I believe Thou hast even at this moment begun to work in me to will and do of Thy good pleasure. I trust Thee utterly, and I trust Thee now."

Are you afraid to take the sudden step, the leap in the dark? If ever you are to enter this glorious land flowing with milk and honey, you must sooner or later step into the brimming waters. There is no other path. To do it now may save you months and even years of disappointment and grief.

PART 2:

DIFFICULTIES

CHAPTER 5
DIFFICULTIES CONCERNING CONSECRATION

Christians must not be ignorant of the temptations that stand ready to oppose every onward step of their progress heavenward. Those temptations are especially active when the soul is awakened to a hunger and thirst after righteousness and begins to reach out after the fullness that is ours in Christ.

The chief temptation that meets the soul and assaults at every step of the pathway is feelings. Because we do not feel God has taken us in hand, we cannot believe He has. We put feelings first, faith second, and fact last although God's invariable rule in everything is, fact first, faith second, and feeling last of all.

Meet this temptation by simply adopting God's

order and putting faith before feeling. Give yourself to the Lord definitely and fully, according to your present light, asking the Holy Spirit to show you all that is contrary to Him in your heart or life. If He shows you anything, give it to Him immediately and say, "Thy will be done." If He does not, believe there is nothing and let faith take hold of this fact. If you are steadfast in this reckoning, the feeling will come.

The way you may have been acting toward God is this: Because you have not felt any change, you have painfully concluded there is none. This sort of perplexity will last forever, unless you cut it short by faith.

The Levitical law of offerings to the Lord settles that everything given to Him becomes, by that very act, something made holy not by the giver's state of mind, but by the holiness of the Divine receiver, set apart from all other things, something that cannot be put to any other uses without sacrilege. All Israel would have been aghast at a man who having given his offering dared stretch forth a hand to retake it. Yet earnest-hearted Christians with no thought of the sacrilege they are committing are guilty of similar acts by giving themselves to the Lord in solemn consecration, then, through unbelief, taking back that which they have given.

Because God is not visibly present to the eye, it is difficult to feel a transaction with Him is real.

Some will say, "Ah, yes; but if He would only

speak to me and say He took me when I gave myself to Him, I would have no trouble believing it." Of course you would not, but where would be the room for faith? Sight, hearing, and feeling are not faith. Believing what we cannot see, hear, or feel, is faith and the Bible tells us our salvation is to be by faith. When we surrender ourselves to the Lord, according to His command, He does then and there receive us, and from that moment we are His.

Deuteronomy 26:17–19 says that on the very day the Israelites avouched the Lord to be their God and to follow Him, He avouched them to be His holy people.

He has commanded us to be entirely surrendered to Him. It is thus we come to know our hearts "purified by faith" and are enabled to live, stand, and walk by faith.

You have trusted the Lord Jesus for the forgiveness of your sins, and know something of what it is to belong to the family of God, and to be made an heir of God through faith in Christ. You long to be conformed to the image of your Lord. You have tried over and over to surrender your whole self to His will, without apparent success. Come once more to Him. Ask Him to reveal hidden rebellion. If He reveals nothing, then believe there is nothing. Believe He has accepted you. You have wholly yielded yourself to the Lord and from henceforth do not in any sense belong to yourself.

Consider it a settled matter. If you begin to question your surrender or God's acceptance, your wavering faith will produce a wavering experience.

You will find it a great help to say over and over, "Lord, I am Yours; I do yield and leave myself entirely to You, and I believe You accept me. Work in me all the good pleasure of Your will, and I will only lie still in Your hands and trust You."

Make this your continual attitude before the Lord. Confess it to yourself, your God, your friends. Sooner or later you will find you are being made into "a holy people unto the Lord, as He hath spoken."

CHAPTER 6
DIFFICULTIES CONCERNING FAITH

The next step in the soul's progress is faith. Again, the soul encounters difficulty and hindrance.

"I know everything in the Christian life is by faith," the seeker says. "That is what makes it so hard. I have no faith. I do not even know what it is, or how to get it." He is plunged into darkness, almost despair.

Your idea of faith may be a religious exercise of soul or an inward, gracious disposition of heart—something tangible you use as a passport to God's favor, or to purchase His gifts. You pray for faith, expecting something like this. Never having received it, you insist you have no faith.

Faith is not in the least like this. It is simply

believing God. As sight is only seeing, so faith is only believing. If you believe the truth, you are saved; if you believe a lie, you are lost. Your salvation comes, not because your faith saves you, but because it links you to the Savior who saves.

Try to imagine yourself acting in your human relations as you do in your spiritual relations. You would not eat, for the cook might have poisoned your food. You would be compelled to walk, lacking trust in conveyances, roads, drivers. You would believe no friends, business agents, or the newspaper. You would say, "I don't believe there's a queen or Ireland, for I have seen neither, and I believe in nothing except what I have seen and felt and touched." Folly!

Ask yourself what greater folly it is when you tell God you have no power to believe His word, "for you have no faith." Is it possible that you can trust your fellowmen and not your God; that you can receive the "witness of men" and cannot receive the "witness of God"; that you commit your dearest earthly interests to weak, failing fellow creatures without a fear and are afraid to commit your spiritual interests to the Savior who laid down His life for you—He who is "able to save to the uttermost all who come unto God by Him"?

You say you cannot believe without the Holy Spirit. Very well; will you conclude your want of faith is because of the failure of the Holy Spirit to do His work? In taking up this position, you are not only "making God a liar," you are showing an utter want of confidence in the Holy Spirit.

We never have to wait for Him. He is always waiting for us. I have such confidence in the Holy Ghost, and in His being always ready to do His work, that I dare to say you can believe at this very moment. Say, "Lord, I will believe, I do believe," and continue to say it.

I remember early in my Christian life, being stirred to the depths by an appeal in a volume of old sermons—that all who loved the Lord Jesus should show how worthy He was of being trusted by the steadfastness of their own faith in Him. I suddenly glimpsed the privilege and glory of being called to walk in paths so dark only an utter recklessness of trust would be possible.

If you can trust Him to manage the universe and all of creation, can your case be so much more complex and difficult that you need to be anxious or troubled about His management of you? Away with such unworthy doubtings! Abandon yourself to the keeping, saving power of the Lord Jesus and never allow yourself to doubt again.

Do not plead, "I cannot trust because I have no faith." Proclaim, "I can trust my Lord, and I will trust Him; and not all the powers of earth or hell shall be able to make me doubt my wonderful, glorious, faithful Redeemer!"

Be patient, trustful, and wait. A time of darkness is only permitted that "the trial of your faith, being much more precious than of gold that perisheth, though it be tried with fire, might be found unto praise and honor and glory at the appearing of Jesus Christ."

CHAPTER 7
DIFFICULTIES CONCERNING
THE WILL

W hen the child of God has stepped out of himself into Christ and begun to know the blessedness of the life hid with Christ in God, he meets one particular difficulty. After the first wonderful emotions of peace and rest have subsided, or if they never came, he begins to question the things he has been passing through. He sees himself as a hypocrite for believing they are real. He is afraid to say he is altogether the Lord's, yet he cannot bring himself to say he is not.

There is nothing here which will not be easily overcome, once the Christian thoroughly understands the principles of the new life and has learned how to live in it. The common thought is, life is to be lived in the emotions. Consequently, all the soul's attention is directed toward them. As they are satisfactory or otherwise, the soul rests or is troubled.

The truth is, life is to be lived not in the emotions, but in the will. Fenelon says that "pure religion resides in the will alone." Our emotions are not ourselves. If God is to take possession of us, He must enter and dwell in the central will or personality. If he reigns there by the power of His Spirit, all the rest of our nature must come under His sway.

A young man of great intelligence, seeking to enter into this new life, was utterly discouraged at finding himself the slave to doubting. When told the secret concerning the will, he exclaimed, "What! Do you mean to tell me I can choose to believe in that bold way, when nothing seems true to me? Will that kind of believing be real?"

"Yes. Simply put your will over on God's side, making up your mind you will believe what He says, because He says it."

The young man solemnly said, "I cannot control my emotions, but I can control my will. If it is only my will that needs to be set straight, I give it to God."

From that moment, he held steadily through all his emotions' pitiful clamoring that accused him of hypocrisy. At the end of his days, he found himself triumphant, every emotion and thought in captivity to the power of the Spirit of God. At times it had drained all his willpower to say he believed, but he kept on. The result has been one of the grandest Christian lives I know of in its marvelous simplicity, directness, and power over sin.

A lady who entered into this life faced a great prospective trial. She used this secret and paid not the slightest attention to her emotions, repeating over and over, "Thy will be done." In an incredibly short time, she began to find even her emotions rejoicing in the will of God.

Another lady had a besetting sin and prayed: "Lord, take possession of my will, and work in me." Immediately, she began to find deliverance, not by the power of an outward commandment, but by the inward power of the Spirit of God.

Cease to consider your emotions; they are only servants. Regard your will, which is your king. When you have got hold of this secret, all the scriptural commands to present yourself as a living sacrifice to Him and abide in Christ become possible.

I am convinced that the Bible expressions concerning the "heart" do not mean the emotions, but our wills, which we are to give up as a child gives up the misdirected will that belongs to it as a child.

Is your face set like a flint to carry out the Father's will? If so, no matter how much your feelings clamor against it, you are the Lord's, and He has begun to work in you.

Pasteur Theodore Monod, of Paris, gives the

experience of a Presbyterian minister, William Hill. "I covenanted to be the Lord's and laid my head upon the altar, a living sacrifice. I rose from my knees, conscious of no change, yet sure I did with all the sincerity and honesty of purpose of which I was capable make an entire and eternal consecration to God. I did not believe God accepted me, yet I desired to do so." He went on to state that not until he found the method of living by the moment did he find rest. He felt shut up to a momentary dependence upon the grace of Christ and refused to allow the adversary to trouble him about past or future but vowed to walk by naked faith. "Since that time the Lord has given me a steady victory over sins which before enslaved me," he wrote. "I have covenanted to walk by faith, and not by feelings."

CHAPTER 8
DIFFICULTIES
CONCERNING GUIDANCE

Y ou have begun the life of faith. You have
given yourself to the Lord to be wholly
His. Your earnest desire is to follow Him. But you
have not yet learned to know the Good Shepherd's
voice and are in great doubt and perplexity as to
what really is His will.

There is a way out for the *fully surrendered* soul.
First, if you *purpose* to obey the Lord in every respect and only need to know His will in order to
consent to it, you surely cannot doubt His willingness to make His will known, and to guide you in
the right paths. James 1:5–6 promises, "If any of
you lack wisdom, let him ask of God, that giveth
to all men liberally, and upbraideth not; and it shall
be given him."

Our faith must confidently look for and expect His guidance. James 1:6–7 warns, "Let him ask in faith, nothing wavering. For he that wavereth is like a wave of the sea driven with the wind and tossed. For let not that man think that he shall receive any thing of the Lord."

Divine guidance has been promised. If you seek it, you are sure to receive it.

Next, remember God has all knowledge and wisdom. He may guide you into paths where He knows great blessings lie but which you feel will result in confusion and loss. His love may lead you to run counter to the loving wishes of even your dearest friends.

How is God's guidance to come to us? How shall we be able to know His voice? In four ways and by the test of harmony; His voice will always be in harmony with itself, no matter in how many ways He speaks. If God tells me something in one voice, He cannot possibly tell me the opposite in another voice.

1. The Scriptures. Until you have found and obeyed God's will as revealed in the Bible, you must not ask nor expect a separate, direct, personal revelation. Listening to an inward voice without having first sought out and obeyed the scriptural rules opens ourselves to error. But remember, the Bible is a book of principles, not one of disjointed aphorisms; so avoid taking Scripture out of context.

2. Convictions of our own higher judgment.

Do not rely on isolated texts, but study the principles of the Bible. If you find none to settle your special point of difficulty, seek guidance in the other ways. God will surely voice Himself to you. Remember, "impressions" can come from sources other than the Holy Spirit: such sources as the strong personalities of those around us, wrong physical conditions, and also our spiritual enemies. It is not enough to have a "leading"; we must find the source of that leading and test it by scriptural teachings and our own spiritually enlightened judgment, "common sense."

Some may say, "But I thought we were not to depend on our human understanding in divine things." We are to depend on human judgment and common sense *enlightened by the Spirit of God*. He will speak to us through the faculties He Himself has given us.

3. Providential circumstances. If a "leading" is of God, He will go before us and open a way for us to follow. It is never a sign of a divine leading when the Christian insists on battering down doors the Lord has not opened.

4. Inward impressions of the Holy Spirit on our minds. If we feel a "stop in our minds," we must wait until this is removed before acting. A steadfast Christian gave me her secret. "I always mind the checks." We must never ignore the voice of our inward impressions.

Neither should we be discouraged when good

and evil meet in the spiritual world opened to our souls. That God cares enough about us to show us how to live is the strongest proof of love He could give.

God's promise is that He will take possession of our will and work in us to do His will; His suggestions come not so much as commands from the outside, as desires springing up within. This makes of service perfect liberty, for it is always easy to do what we desire to do. He "writes His laws on our hearts and our minds," so we are drawn to obey, instead of being driven to it.

If the divine sense of "oughtness" does not come, stand still, and refrain from action, until He gives you light. If the suggestion is from Him, it will continue and strengthen; if not, it will disappear. You may find the doubt has been His warning voice, or temptation, or morbid feelings.

Take your perplexities to the Lord and ask Him to make plain His will for you.

Promise to obey and believe implicitly He is guiding you. Let everything else go that it might be yours.

CHAPTER 9
DIFFICULTIES
CONCERNING DOUBTS

A great many Christians are slaves to doubting; not the existence of God, or the truths of the Bible, but their own personal relations with the God in whom they profess to believe. They doubt the forgiveness of their sins, hopes of heaven, and their own inward experience. Their lives are made wretched, their usefulness hindered, and their communion with God broken.

It seems strange that people with the name Believers should confess they have doubts. Yet most Christians, including those who have made many steps toward the life and walk of faith, have resigned themselves to their malady as a part of the necessary discipline of earthly life. They look on themselves in the light of martyrs and groan under spiritual conflicts that should better be called spiritual rebellions!

Just as well might I join in with the laments of a drunkard and unite with him in prayer for grace to endure the discipline of his fatal appetite, as to give way for one instant to the weak complaints of those enslaved to doubt, and try to console them under their slavery. To one and the other, I would dare do nothing but proclaim the perfect deliverance which the Lord Jesus Christ has in store for them and beseech them with all the power at my command, to be free.

A mother once left her two little girls with me while doing errands. One sang; the other sat alone in a corner, doubting whether her mother would come back to her. At last, she worked herself into a frenzy, for fear her mother would be glad of the chance to get rid of her. I shall not easily forget the grief, wounded love, indignation, and pity in the mother's face when she returned.

Have you tasted the luxury of indulging in hard thoughts against those you think have wounded you? Have you known the positive fascination brooding over their wrongs brings? Just like this is the luxury of doubting. You do not mean to blame or accuse God of indifference, because you feel you are unworthy. You believe you are doubting yourself; you are really doubting Him.

Jesus said, "What man of you, having a hundred sheep, if he lose one of them, doth not leave the ninety and nine in the wilderness, and go after that which is lost until he finds it?"

Doubts and discouragement are all from an evil source, and always untrue.

Deliverance from the fatal habit of doubting is found only in Christ, the same as deliverance from any other sin. Hand your doubting over to Him, as you would your pride or temper. Take a pledge against it, as you would urge the drunkard to do against drink, trusting in the Lord alone to keep you steadfast. Then let the doubts clamor; they cannot hurt you if you will not let them. When we surrender doubting as an act of will, His blessed Spirit will begin to work, and we shall find ourselves kept from doubting by His mighty and overcoming power.

I have often awakened to a perfect army of doubts clamoring at my door for admittance. I have been compelled to lift up the "shield of faith" and hand the whole army over to the Lord to conquer, saying, "I dare not doubt; I must trust. God is my Father, and He does love me. Jesus saves me; He saves me now." The victory has always been complete.

Dear doubting souls, go and do likewise and a similar victory shall be yours. Turn from your doubts with horror, as you would from blasphemy; for they are blasphemy. You cannot hinder doubts from coming, any more than you can hinder boys in the street from swearing at you. But just as you can refuse to listen to the boys or join in their oaths, so you can refuse to listen to or join in with the doubts.

Write out your determination never to doubt again. Trust the Lord to keep you from failing. Never let your faith waver. Sooner or later you will know it is true, and all doubts will vanish in the blaze of the glory of the absolute faithfulness of God!

Doubts and discouragements are, I believe, inlets by which evil enters, while faith is an impregnable wall against all evil. Deliverance lies at your very door. Try it, and see. "According to your faith" it shall inevitably be unto you.

CHAPTER 10
DIFFICULTIES
CONCERNING TEMPTATIONS

Certain great mistakes are made concerning the matter of temptation in the practical working out of the life of faith.

First, people seem to expect that after the soul has entered into rest in the Lord, temptations will cease; they think the promised deliverance is to be not only from yielding to temptation, but also even from being tempted.

Next, they make the mistake of looking upon temptation as sin, and of blaming themselves for suggestions of evil, even while they abhor them. This brings them into condemnation and discouragement; and discouragement, if continued in, always ends at last in actual sin. Sin makes an easy prey of a discouraged soul; so that we fall often from the very fear of having fallen.

To meet the first of these difficulties, it is only necessary to refer to the Scripture declarations which state the Christian life is to be throughout a warfare; and that it is to be especially so when we are "seated in heavenly places in Christ Jesus." We are called to wrestle against spiritual enemies, whose power and skill to tempt us must doubtless be far superior to any we have heretofore encountered.

When the children of Israel first left Egypt, the Lord did not lead them the nearest way, through the land of the Philistines, "Lest peradventure the people repent when they see war, and they return to Egypt." Afterwards, when they had learned how to trust Him better, He permitted their enemies to attack. Moreover, even in their wilderness journey they met with but few enemies and fought but few battles, compared to those they encountered in the land of Canaan—where they found seven great nations and thirty-one kings to be conquered, besides walled cities to be taken, and giants to be overcome.

They could not have fought these until they had gone into the land where the enemies were. The very power of your temptations may perhaps be one of the strongest proofs that you are really in the land of promise you have been seeking to enter; you must never allow them to cause you to question the fact of your having entered it.

The second mistake is harder to deal with. Temptation is not sin, yet much distress arises from not understanding this fact. The enemy whispers doubts, blasphemies, jealousies, envyings, and pride, then turns round and says, "Oh, how wicked you must be to think such things! It is very plain you are not trusting the Lord; if you had been, it would be impossible for these things to have entered your heart."

One of the most fatal things in the life of faith is discouragement; one of the most helpful is confidence. A wise man once said that in overcoming temptations confidence was the first thing, the second, and the third. We must expect to conquer. That is why the Lord said so often to Joshua, "Be strong. . .not afraid. . .neither be thou dismayed."

Discouragement arises sometimes from what we think is righteous grief and disgust at ourselves that things are temptations, but it is really mortification that we have been secretly self-congratulating ourselves that we are too pure for such things to tempt us. A result of self-love, the mortification and discouragement are not humility, but a far worse condition than the temptation itself.

An allegory illustrates this wonderfully. Satan called a council to consult how they might make a good man sin. One evil spirit said he would set before the man the pleasures of sin, its delights and rich rewards. Another said he would tell him of the pains and sorrows of virtue. Satan shook his head. "Ah, no, those ways have been tried, and he knows better." The third imp gave the winning suggestion: to discourage the man's soul and conquer through discouragement.

A lady once came to me under great darkness, simply from not understanding. She had been living happily in the life of faith, so free from temptation, she thought she would never be tempted again. She had lived a sheltered, innocent life; now her thoughts horrified her. She began to believe she had never been born again. I told her she was no more to blame for the dreadful thoughts than she could help a wicked man pouring out blasphemies in her presence. I urged her to recognize and treat them as such. She grasped the truth, faced the enemy, and called on the Lord to deliver her, which He did.

The way of victory over temptation is faith. It seems impossible to believe the Lord can or will manage our temptations without our help, but we must put them into His hands and leave them there.

We must then commit ourselves as certainly to the Lord for victory over our temptations, as we committed ourselves at first for forgiveness; and we must leave ourselves just as utterly in His hands for one as for the other.

Thousands of God's children have done this and can testify today that marvelous victories have been gained for them over numberless temptations, and that they have in very truth been made "more than conquerors" through Him who loves them.

CHAPTER 11
DIFFICULTIES
CONCERNING FAILURES

T he very title of this chapter may perhaps startle some. "Failures," they will say; "we thought there were no failures in this life of faith!"

There ought not to be, and need not be; but there sometimes are, and we must deal with facts, and not with theories. There are few, if any, who do not confess they have at times been overcome by at least a momentary temptation.

In speaking of sin here, I mean conscious, known sin, not the sins of ignorance, or the inevitable sin of our nature, which are all met by the provisions of Christ and do not disturb our fellowship with God.

I once saw a baby girl playing about the library, while her father was resting on the lounge. A pretty inkstand on the table took the child's fancy. She climbed on a chair and secured it. Walking over to her father with an air of childish triumph, she turned it upside down on his white shirt and laughed with glee as she saw the black streams trickling down.

This was a very wrong thing for the child to do, but it could not be called sin, for she knew no better.

When a believer finds himself surprised into sin, he is tempted either to be discouraged and give everything up as lost, or cover his sin up, by calling it infirmity, and refusing to be candid and aboveboard about it. Either course is equally fatal to the life of holiness. He must face the sad fact at once, call the thing by its right name, and discover, if possible, the reason and the remedy. This life of union with God requires the utmost honesty with Him and with ourselves.

A sudden failure is no reason for ceasing to trust, but only an unanswerable argument why we must trust more fully than ever. Neither is the integrity of our doctrine touched by it. We are not preaching a *state*, but a *walk*; not a *place*, but a *way*.

As well might a child learning to walk lies down in despair when he has fallen and refuses to take another step, as a believer who gives up in despair because of having fallen into sin. Both must get right up and try again. When the children of Israel met with a disastrous defeat, even Joshua, the faithful, wailed to the Lord, who said unto him, "Get thee up; wherefore liest thou upon thy face?"

A little girl once expressed, with a child's outspoken candor, the belief we must suffer for a time —even though I had assured her the Lord Jesus always forgave our sins the minute we asked Him.

She *said* what most Christians *think,* and worse, act on. Yet it is totally contrary to what parents desire from their children. Consider the mother who grieves when her naughty child goes off alone and doubts her willingness to forgive. How her heart goes out in welcoming love to the repentant little one who runs to her at once and begs her forgiveness!

If our eyes are turned away from Jesus to look upon our own sin and weakness, we shall leave the path at once. The believer who trusts must do as the children of Israel did, rise up "*early* in the morning" and "*run*" to the place where the evil thing is hidden, take it out of its hiding place, and lay it "out before the Lord." He must confess his sin, stone it, burn it, bury it, and raise over it a great heap of stones, that it might be forever hidden from his sight. He must claim by faith an immediate forgiveness and cleansing and go on trusting harder and more absolutely than ever.

An earnest Christian worker living for several months in peace and joy was suddenly overcome by the temptation to treat a brother unkindly. His health failed, and he spent three years of utter misery, away from God. Then he met a Christian lady who said, "You sinned and should not try to excuse it. But have you never confessed to the Lord and asked Him to forgive you?"

"Confessed!" he exclaimed. "I have done nothing but confess it all these years, but I never felt He forgave me."

She quoted 1 John 1:9, "If we confess our sins, he is faithful and just to forgive us our sins, and to cleanse us from all unrighteousness." He realized what doubting had done. His darkness vanished, and he rejoiced in the fullness of His salvation.

The causes of failure lie in anything—no matter how insignificant, or deeply hidden—which is contrary to the will of God but cherished in the heart. Our blessed Guide, the indwelling Holy Spirit, is always secretly showing these things to us by pangs of conscience, so we are left without excuse.

We once moved to a new house. I found a clean-looking cider-cask in the cellar. It would have been hard to get it upstairs, so I left it. Yet with each spring cleaning I had the feeling my house would not be quite clean until I investigated the innocent-looking cask. Moths began to fill our house, threatening to ruin everything we had. I cleaned carpets, and had furniture reupholstered, to no avail. At last I had the cask opened. Thousands of moths poured out.

In the same way, we must confess every innocent-looking habit or indulgence, every secret corner kept locked against the entrance of the Lord, and "serve Him without fear, in holiness and righteousness—all the days of our life."

CHAPTER 12
IS GOD IN EVERYTHING?

One of the greatest obstacles in life is the difficulty of seeing God in everything. People say, "I can easily submit to things that come from God; but I cannot submit to man, and most of my trials and crosses come through somebody's failure, ignorance, carelessness, or sin."

We know God cannot be the author of these things; and yet, unless He is the agent in the matter, how can we say to Him about it, "Thy will be done?" Moreover, things in which we can see God's hand always have a sweetness in them that consoles while it wounds; but the trials inflicted by man are full of nothing but bitterness.

The question confronts us. "Is God in everything? Have we any warrant from the Scripture for receiving everything from His hands, without regarding the second causes that may have been instrumental in bringing them about?" I answer unhesitatingly, *Yes.* To the children of God, everything comes directly from their Father's hand, no matter who or what may have been the apparent agents. There are no "second causes" for them.

What is needed, then, is to see God in everything with no intervention of second causes. It is to just this we must be brought, before we can know an abiding experience of entire abandonment, and perfect trust. Our abandonment must be to God, not to man; and our trust must be in Him, not in any arm of flesh, or we shall fail at the first trial.

"He hath said, I will never leave thee nor forsake thee. So that we may boldly say, the Lord is my helper, and I will not fear what man shall do unto me." These Scriptures and others like them forever settle the question.

If a child is in his father's arms, nothing can touch him without that father's consent, unless he is too weak to prevent it. Even if this is the case, he suffers the harm first in his own person before he allows it to reach his child. How much more will our heavenly Father, whose love is infinitely greater, and whose strength and wisdom can never be baffled, care for us!

Take Joseph. What could have seemed more apparent sin, and utterly contrary to the will of God, than the actions of his brethren selling him into slavery? Yet Joseph said, "As for you, ye thought evil against me; but God meant it unto good." By the time the brethren's sin reached Joseph, it had become God's will for him, and the greatest blessing in his whole life.

I learned this lesson, long years before I knew the scriptural truth concerning it. A strange lady rose in a prayer meeting. I wondered who she could be, little thinking she was to bring a message to my soul which would teach me a grand, practical lesson. She said she had great difficulty living the life of faith, because of the second causes that seemed to control everything that concerned her. She began to earnestly ask God if He were really in everything. After a few days of such praying, she had what she described as a vision. She thought she was in a perfectly dark place. From a distance, a body of light advanced, surrounded, and enveloped her, saying as it approached, "This is the presence of God!" While so surrounded, all the great and awful things in life seemed to pass before her—fighting armies, wicked men, raging beasts, storms, pestilences, sin and suffering of every kind. She shrank back in terror but soon saw the presence of God so surrounded her that not a lion could reach out its paw, nor a bullet fly through the air, except as the presence of God moved out of the way to permit it. Not a hair of her head could be ruffled, nor anything touch her behind the thin film of the glorious Presence, except as it divided to let the evil through.

Then all the small annoyances of life passed before her. Again, she was so enveloped in the presence of God, not a cross look, harsh word, or petty trial could affect her, unless God's encircling presence moved out of the way to let it. Her question was answered forever.

I once heard of a poor woman who earned a precarious living by daily labor but was a joyous, triumphant Christian. "Ah, Nancy," said a gloomy Christian lady, who both disapproved of and envied her constant cheerfulness. "It is well enough to be happy now, but I should think thoughts of the future would sober you. Suppose you should get sick and be unable to work, or—"

"Stop!" Nancy cried. "I never supposes. The Lord is my Shepherd, and I knows I shall not want. And honey, it's all them supposes as is makin' you so mis'able. You'd better give them all up and just trust the Lord."

A bottle *holds* medicine, a mother *gives* it to a beloved child. Those around us are often the bottles, but the Great Physician pours out the medicine and compels us to drink it.

Shall we rebel against the human bottles? Or say joyfully, "Thy will be done"? If the will of God is our will, and if He always has His way, then in the life of trust, we always have our way also. He who sides with God cannot fail to win in every encounter; and whether the result shall be joy or sorrow, failure or success, death or life, we may under all circumstances join in the apostle's shout of victory, "Thanks be unto God, which always causeth us to triumph in Christ!"

PART 3:

RESULTS

CHAPTER 13
BONDAGE OR LIBERTY

There are two kinds of Christian experience. In *bondage*, the soul is a servant who works for hire. Controlled by a stern sense of duty, he obeys the laws of God, either from fear of punishment or from expectation of wages. In *liberty*, the only right and normal condition, he is a son. He works out the will of the divine Life-giver in love, without fear of punishment or hope of reward.

We cannot shut our eyes to the sad condition of bondage in which so many of God's children live. The reason is legality. The remedy is Christ.

We find in Galatians, some Jewish brethren had come among the churches, representing that certain forms and ceremonies were necessary to their salvation, trying to draw believers from the liberty of the gospel. Peter had united with these teachers. Paul reproves both.

Neither Peter nor the Galatians committed moral sin, but they committed spiritual sin by seeking to substitute works for faith.

We are continually tempted to forget it is not what men *do* that is the vital matter, but rather what they *are*. God is a great deal more concerned about our being "new creatures" in Christ Jesus than anything else. If we are right inwardly, we shall certainly do right outwardly.

Paul was grieved that the Galatians made the mistake of thinking something else besides Christ was necessary for their right Christian living.

Jewish Christians added ceremonial law; we add resolutions, agonizing, Christian work, church-going, etc. It does not make much difference what you add; the wrong thing is to add anything to Christ at all.

A few of the many contrasts between legality and Christian liberty follow.

The law says, this do and thou shalt live. . . Make you a new heart and spirit. The gospel says, Live, and then thou shalt do. . .a new heart I will give you, and a new spirit will I put within you.

The law says, Thou shalt love the Lord thy God with all thy heart, soul, and mind. The gospel says, Herein is love, not that we loved God, but that He loved us and sent His son to be the propitiation for our sins.

The law says, The wages of sin is death. The gospel says, The gift of God is eternal life through

Jesus Christ our Lord.

Under the law, salvation was wages. Under the gospel, salvation is a gift.

Paul tells us the law "is our schoolmaster," not our savior. After faith in Christ is come, we are no longer to be under a schoolmaster. "Wherefore," he says, "thou art no more a servant, but a son."

Suppose a servant who has done her paid duty is offered the master's love and lifted from servanthood to be his bride. At once the whole spirit changes. She serves her husband, not her master.

What if she feels so unworthy that the old sense of working for wages causes her spirit to again call the man master, not husband? Nothing so destroys the sweetness of any relation as the creeping in of the legal spirit, the moment when duties are performed from duty and not love. Christians continually say this to God. Legal Christians do not deny Christ, but to add anything at all is to deny His completeness. A religion of bondage always exalts self. A religion of liberty knows it is all Christ.

A friend's life demonstrated this. She worked harder for her salvation than any slave ever worked to purchase his freedom.

"What would you think of children forced to agonize and wrestle with their parents every morning for necessary food and clothing?" I asked. "Or sheep that had to struggle with their shepherd to receive necessary care?"

"It would be all wrong, but why, then, do I have such good times after going through the conflicts and coming to the point of trusting the Lord?"

"Suppose you come to that point to begin with?" I suggested. She admitted she had never until that moment thought she might!

The spirit of bondage makes Christians think our Lord is a "hard master." So used to carrying a "yoke of bondage," whenever they find themselves "walking at liberty" they begin to think there must be something wrong!

Sometimes I think the whole secret of the Christian life is revealed in the child relationship; to believe God is as good a Father as the ideal earthly father. Children do not need to carry in their pockets money for their support. Christians need not have all their spiritual possessions in their own keeping. It is far better for riches to be stored in Christ, and receive it direct from His hands.

Sometimes a great mystery is made of the life hid with Christ in God. Liberty makes it plain we are "no more servants, but sons" and, "against such there is no law." The man who lives by the power of an inward righteous nature fulfills the law in his soul and is free. The other rebels and is bound. Abandon yourselves so utterly to the Lord Jesus Christ that He may deliver you from every law that could possibly enslave you.

CHAPTER 14
GROWTH

One great objection made against those who advocate this life of faith is that they do not teach a growth in grace. They are supposed to teach the soul arrives in one moment at a state of perfection, beyond which there is no advance, and all the scriptural exhortations that point toward growth and development are rendered void by this teaching.

Since exactly the opposite is true, I will try to show what seems to me the scriptural way of growing, and in what place the soul must be in order to grow.

2 Peter 3:18, "But grow in grace, and in the knowledge of our Lord and Saviour Jesus Christ," expresses exactly what we who teach this life of faith believe to be God's will for us, and what He has made it possible for us to experience. We believe in

a growing that produces ripe fruit. We expect to reach the aim set before us. No parent would be satisfied with the growth of his child if year after year it remained the same helpless babe as when born. Neither would a farmer feel comfortable should his corn stop short at the blade and never produce full ears. Growth, to be real, must be progressive.

I knew a lady once who had been growing for twenty-five years, and I asked how much more unworldly and devoted to the Lord she was now than when she began her Christian life. "Alas," she confessed. "I fear I am not nearly so much so."

The trouble with her and others is, they are trying to grow into grace, instead of in it, like a withered rosebush planted in a hard, stony path, with a view to growing into the flower bed. When the children of Israel began their travels at Kadesh Barnea, they stood at the borders of the promised land. Forty years later, in the plains of Moab, they were also at its borders, only with a river to cross which at first there would not have been. In order to get possession of the land, it was necessary to first be in it. In order to grow in grace, we must first be planted in grace's fruitful soil, tended by a divine Husbandman and warmed by the Sun of Righteousness, to bring forth much fruit.

Grace is the unhindered, wondrous, boundless love of God, poured out upon us in an infinite variety of ways, not according to our deserving, but His measureless heart of love. Put together the most deep, tender love you have felt, multiply by infinity, and you will faintly glimpse the love and grace of God! To grow in grace means being planted in the very heart of this divine love, to put ourselves in His hands and leave it with Him; to grow as lilies and babes, with neither care nor anxiety. Even Solomon in all his glory was not so arrayed.

The slightest barrier between your soul and Christ may cause you to dwindle and fade, as a plant in a cellar or under a bushel. Our divine Husbandman can turn any soil into the soil of grace the moment we place ourselves in His hands. He does not need to transplant us.

We need to learn the flowers' secret; to grow, but only in God's way, not hindering Him with our own anxious efforts. What the flower is by nature, we must be by an intelligent and free surrender. Self must step aside to let God work. "Consider the lilies, *how they grow;* they toil not, neither do they spin." *Let* yourself grow. Abide in the Vine, so the divine Husbandman, who makes the very desert bloom as a rose, can prune and purge and water and tend you that you may bring forth fruit. What a picture of life and growth far different from the ordinary life and growth of Christians—a life of rest, and growth without effort, and yet a life and growth crowned with glorious results.

We may rest assured that all the resources of God's infinite grace will be brought to bear on the growing of the tiniest flower in His spiritual garden, as certainly as they are in His earthly creation. The violet abides peacefully in its little place, content to receive its daily portion without concerning itself about the wandering of the winds, or the falling of the rain. So must we repose in the present moment, as it comes to us from God.

This is the kind of "growth in grace" we who have entered into the life of full trust believe. We rejoice to know there are, growing up now in the Lord's heritage, many such plants, who as the lilies behold the face of the sun and grow thereby are, by "beholding as in a glass the glory of the Lord," being changed into the same image from glory to glory, even as by the Spirit of the Lord.

They grow rapidly and with such success because they are not concerned about their growing and are hardly conscious they do grow. Their Lord has told them to abide, and they shall certainly bring forth much fruit. They are content to leave the cultivating, growing, training and pruning, to their good Husbandman.

Let us look at the subject practically. Growing is not a thing of effort, but the result of an inward life-principle of growth. A dead oak cannot be made to grow by stretching and pulling. A live oak grows without stretching. It is plain, therefore, that the essential thing is to get within you the "life hid with Christ in God," the wonderful divine life of an indwelling Holy Spirit. Be filled with this, and whether you are conscious of it or not, you cannot help growing. Say "yes" to your Father's will and "the peace that passeth understanding" shall keep your hearts and minds through Christ Jesus.

CHAPTER 15
SERVICE

There is, perhaps, no part of Christian experience where a greater change is known, upon entering into this life hid with Christ in God, than in the matter of service.

Service is apt to be bondage, done purely as a matter of duty, often as a trial and a cross. Things at first a joy and delight become weary tasks.

One dear Christian expressed it well: "I was so full of joy and love when I was first converted that I was only too glad and thankful to be allowed to do anything for my Lord, and I eagerly entered every open door. But after awhile my early joy faded, my love burned less fervently. I began to wish I had not been so eager, for I found myself in lines of service distasteful and burdensome. Once begun, I could not very well give them up yet longed to do so. I was expected to visit the sick, and pray beside their bed; to attend prayer meetings, and speak at them; in short, to be always ready for every effort in Christian work. The sense of these expectations bowed me down until I would have infinitely preferred scrubbing all day on my hands and knees, to being compelled to go through the treadmill of my daily Christian work."

Is this your experience? Have you gone to your work as a slave to his daily task, believing it your duty, but rebounding back like an India-rubber ball into your real interests and pleasures the moment your work was over?

Another picture may better describe your case. You do love your work in the abstract but encounter so many cares and responsibilities, misgivings and doubts as to your capacity to carry it out, it becomes a heavy burden and you are weary before the labor is begun. You continually distress yourself about the results.

The soul that fully enters into the blessed life of faith is entirely delivered from these forms of bondage. Service becomes delightful because, having surrendered its will into the keeping of the Lord, He works in it, and the soul finds itself *wanting* to do the things God wants it to do. If a man's *will* is really set on a thing, he can laugh at opposition and scorn the thought of any "cross" connected with it!

The way we look at things determines whether we think they are crosses or not. Believers need to *want* to do God's will as much as other people want to do their own will. It is what God intended and promised. "I will put my laws into their mind, and write them in their hearts," He says in Hebrews 8:6–13. We, who are a stiff-necked people, always rebel against a law from outside of us, while we joyfully embrace the same law springing up within. God's way of working is to get possession of a man's will and work it for him.

If you are in bondage in the matter of service, surrender entire control to Him. A certain lady rebelled for years against a little act of service she knew was right but hated. Out of the depths of despair, she prayed, "*Thy will be done.*" In one short hour, that thing began to look sweet and precious to her. It is wonderful what miracles God works in wills utterly surrendered to Him.

There is also deliverance in the wonderful life of faith from burdens carried in connection with even beloved service. The Lord is our burden-bearer; upon Him we must lay off every care. What have we to do with thinking whether we are fit or not? The Master-workman has the right to use any tool He pleases; it is plainly not the business of the tool to decide whether it is the right one. In our utter helplessness, His strength is made perfect. No wonder Paul could say, "I glory in my infirmities, that the power of Christ may rest upon me."

If the work is His, the responsibility is also His, and we have no room left for worrying about the results. The most effectual workers are those who do not feel anxiety about their work but commit it all to their dear Master, trusting Him to guide them in it moment by moment.

The life of trust also delivers us by reminding us no individual is responsible for all the work in the world, only for a small share. I may have five, or two, or only one talent. I am to do that which I am called to do, nothing more.

A young Christian, sent to speak a message to one soul she met on a walk, supposed she must speak to everyone she met while walking, a perpetual obligation and an impossible task. A friend told her to put herself under the Lord's guidance and trust Him to point out each particular person to whom He would have her speak. He assured her He never puts forth His sheep without going before them. This freed her from bondage, and she was able to do much blessed work for her Master without worry or care.

Years ago, I ran across this sentence in an old book: "Never indulge, at the close of an action, in. . .self-congratulation or self-despair. Forget the things that are behind, the moment they are past, leaving them with God." To sum it all up, put your work into the Lord's hands and leave it there. Even in the midst of a life of ceaseless activity, you shall "find rest to your soul" and be an "instrument of righteousness."

CHAPTER 16
PRACTICAL RESULTS IN THE DAILY WALK AND CONVERSATION

If all that has been written in the foregoing chapters on the life hid with Christ be true, its results in the practical daily walk and conversation ought to be marked. The people who have entered into the enjoyment of it ought to be a peculiar people, zealous of good works.

My son, now with God, once wrote to a friend something to this effect: that we are God's witnesses necessarily, because the world will not read the Bible, but they will read our lives. Upon the report these give, will depend their belief in the divine nature of the religion we possess. If our religion is to make any headway, it must be proved to be more than a theory; we must present to the investigation of critical minds the realities of lives transformed by the mighty power of God, "working in them all the good pleasure of His will."

I desire, therefore, to speak very solemnly of the necessary fruits of a life of faith, and to press home to the hearts of my readers their personal responsibility to "walk worthy of the high calling," wherewith they have been called. The standard of practical holy living has been so low among Christians that the least degree of real devotedness of life and walk is looked upon with surprise and often even with disapprobation by a large portion of the church. For the most part, the followers of the Lord Jesus Christ are satisfied with a life so conformed to the world, and so like it in almost every respect, that, to a casual observer, no difference is discernible.

We who have heard the call of our God to a life of entire consecration and perfect trust must come out from the world and be separate. We must set our affections on heavenly things, not on earthly ones. We must walk through the world as Christ walked and have the mind that is in Him. We must abstain from all appearance of evil and do everything, not for our own glory, but for the glory of God. To sum it all up, since He who called us is holy, so we must be holy in all matter of conversation.

Some Christians seem to think all the requirements of a holy life are met because they do so much for the Lord in public. They feel a liberty to be cross and ugly and un-Christlike in private. But we must be just as Christlike to our servants as we are to our minister. In daily homely living, practical piety can best show itself, and we may well question any "professions" that fail under this test of daily life. Cross, anxious, discouraged, gloomy, complaining, doubting, exacting, selfish, cruel, hard-hearted, self-indulgent Christians, or those with sharp tongues or bitter spirits may be earnest in their work and have honorable places in the church but they are not Christlike Christians.

The life hid with Christ in God must not be hidden as to practical results. We must prove we "possess" that which we "profess." We must turn our backs on everything that is contrary to the perfect will of God and be a "peculiar people," in both God's and the world's eyes. We must look on our money and energy as belonging to the Lord and to be used by Him, recognizing that if we seek first the kingdom of God and His righteousness, all needful things will be added unto us. Our days will be spent in serving God and others, not ourselves and whatever we do will be done, "not with eye-service, as men-pleasers, but as the servants of Christ, doing the will of God from the heart."

Into all this we shall be led by the Spirit of God. Meekness and quietness of spirit become in time the characteristics of a surrendered life. So do absence of worry, or anxiety, deliverance from care and fear, a lack of sensitivity to slights and affronts, calmness in the midst of turmoil, and a yielding to the wishes of others. God's glory and the welfare of His creatures become the absorbing delight of the soul, and those who ever grow more like Christ wear in their faces evidence of the beautiful, inward divine life.

Have you become conscious of the voice of God speaking to you in the depths of your soul? Have you begun to feel uneasy with some of your habits and pursuits? Have not paths of devotedness and service opened before you, with the longing thought, "Oh, that I could walk in them." The heights of Christian perfection can only be reached by each moment faithfully following the Guide who is to lead you there; He leads the way one step at a time, in the little things of our daily lives. Obey Him perfectly the moment you are sure of His will.

I knew a soul given up to follow the Lord whithersoever He might lead her, who in a very little while traveled from the depths of darkness and despair, into the consecration of herself to the Lord that He might work in her will. Her swift obedience made her life a testimony to those around her; even some who began by opposing and disbelieving were forced to acknowledge it was of God and were won to a similar surrender. If you would know a like blessing, abandon yourself to the guidance of your divine Master, and shrink from no surrender for which He may call.

Things small to you may be the key and clue to the deepest springs of your being. No life can be complete that fails in its little things. A look, a word, a tone of voice even, however small they may seem, are often vitally important to God.

Whether you know it or not, this and nothing less is what your consecration meant: inevitable obedience, that the will of your God was to be your will. You did surrender your liberty of choice in an hourly following whithersoever He might lead you, without any turning back.

Let everything else go, that you may live out in a practical daily walk and conversation the Christ-life you have dwelling within you. Day by day you will find Him molding and fashioning you, as you are able to bear it; and become an "epistle of Christ, known and read of all men." Your light shall shine so brightly that men seeing, not you, but your good works, shall glorify, not you, but your Father in heaven.

CHAPTER 17
THE JOY OF OBEDIENCE

Having spoken of some of the difficulties in this life of faith, let me now speak of some of its joys. Foremost among these stands the joy of obedience.

Long ago I read, "Perfect obedience would be perfect happiness, if only we had perfect confidence in the power we were obeying."

This rest has been revealed to me now, not as a vision, but as a reality. I have seen in the Lord Jesus the Master to whom we may yield up our implicit obedience, and, taking His yoke upon us, find our perfect rest.

You little know, hesitating soul, of the joy you are missing. The Master has revealed Himself to you and is calling for your complete surrender, and you shrink and hesitate. You are afraid of an utter abandonment, thinking it involves too much and is too great a risk. You see other souls who seem to walk with easy consciences in a far wider path than that which appears marked out for you.

Many relations in life require from the different parties only moderate degrees of devotion. There is not enough between to make separation an especial distress. In other relations, friendship becomes love. Two hearts give themselves in a union of soul. Separate interests and paths are no longer possible. The deepest desire of each heart is that it may know every secret wish and longing of the other, in order to fly on the wings of the wind to gratify it.

Do such as these not glory in the very obligations and inwardly pity the poor far-off ones who dare not come so near? If you have ever loved any of your fellow human beings enough to find sacrifice and service on their behalf a joy, a whole-souled abandonment of your will to the will of another has gleamed across you as a blessed gift and longed-for privilege, or sweet and precious reality. I would entreat you to let it be so toward Christ, who rejoices over you as a bridegroom over his bride. He has given you all and asks for all in return.

If you are hearing the loving voice of your Lord calling you to Himself in separation from all else, will you shrink or hesitate? No! You will spring out to meet His will with an eager joy and glory in the narrowness of the path He marks out for you. The perfect happiness of perfect obedience will dawn upon your soul, and you will begin to know something of what Jesus meant when He said, "I delight to do Thy will, O My God."

Do you think this joy will be all on your side? My friend, we are not able to understand the delight, satisfaction, and joy our Lord has in us. That we need Him is easy to comprehend; that He needs us seems incomprehensible. He is continually knocking at every heart, asking, "Wilt thou have Me? May I have My way with thee in all things? Wilt thou accept Me for thy heavenly Bridegroom, and leave all others to cleave only unto Me?"

In a thousand ways, He makes this offer of union with Himself to every believer. But all do not say "Yes" to Him. Other loves and interests seem to them too precious to be cast aside. They do not miss the joy of heaven because of this, but they miss an unspeakable present joy.

You are not one of these. From the very first, your soul has cried out eagerly and gladly to all His offers, "Yes, Lord, yes!" The life of love you have entered gives you the right to a lavish outpouring of your all upon your beloved One. Your Lord can make known His secrets, and to you He looks for an instant response to every requirement of His love.

It is wonderful, the glorious, unspeakable privilege upon which you have entered! How little it will matter if men shall hate you and shall separate you from their company and shall reproach you and cast out your name as evil for His dear sake!

You may well "rejoice in that day and leap for joy," for behold, your reward is great in heaven; for if you are a partaker of His suffering, you shall also be of His glory.

In you He sees the "travail of His soul" and is satisfied. Your love and devotedness are His precious reward for all He has done for you, unspeakably sweet to Him. Do not be afraid, then, to let yourself go in a heart-whole devotedness to your Lord that can brook no reserves. Let Him have all of you, body, soul, mind, spirit, time, talents, voice, everything. Do not let there be a day, nor an hour, in which you are not consciously doing His will and following Him wholly.

Christ, while on earth, declared there was no blessedness equal to the blessedness of obedience. More blessed even than to have been the earthly mother of our Lord, to have carried Him in our arms and nourished Him in our bosoms, is to hear and obey His will!

May our surrendered hearts reach out with eager delight to discover and embrace the lovely will of our loving God!

CHAPTER 18
DIVINE UNION

All the dealings of God with the soul of the believer are in order to bring it into oneness with Himself, "That they all may be one; as thou, Father, art in me, and I in thee, that they also may be one in us."

This divine union was the glorious purpose in the heart of God for His people, before the foundation of the world, accomplished in the death of Christ.

God has not hidden it nor made it hard; but the eyes of many are too dim, their hearts too unbelieving for them to grasp it. It is for the purpose of bringing His people into the personal and actual realization of this that the Lord calls upon them so earnestly and repeatedly to abandon themselves to Him.

Consider the disciples. First they were awakened

to their condition and need. They came to Christ, gave their allegiance, and followed. They worked for and believed in Him—yet how unlike Him they were! They knew Christ as outside of them; their Lord and Master, but not yet their life.

Then came Pentecost. These same disciples came to know Him as inwardly revealed. Henceforth He was to them Christ within, working in them to will and do His good pleasure, delivering them, by the law of the Spirit of His life, from bondage to the law of sin and death under which they had been held. No longer was it a war of wills and clashing of interests. His will alone animated them; one interest alone was dear to them. They were made one with Him.

Perhaps you may not have reached this final stage. You may have left much to follow Christ, believed on Him, worked and loved Him, yet not be like Him.

That you may be sure divine union is really intended for you, read passages such as 1 Corinthians 3:16, "Know ye not that ye are the temple of God, and that the Spirit of God dwelleth in you?" Then look at the opening of the chapter. You will see this unspeakably glorious mystery of an indwelling God is the possession of even the weakest and most failing believer in Christ. Every believer's "body is the temple of the Holy Ghost." But unless the believer knows it and lives in the power of it, it is to him as though it were not.

It is a fatal mistake to make our emotions a test of our oneness with Christ. Joyous emotions may delude me into thinking I have entered the divine union when I have not; if I have no emotions, I may grieve over my failure to enter, when I already have.

Character is the only real test. God is holy and those who are one with Him will be holy, also. Our Lord expressed His oneness with the Father thus: "The Son can do nothing of Himself, but what he seeth the Father do: for what things soever He doeth, these also doeth the Son likewise." Christ's test, then, was the fact He did the works of the Father. I know of no other test for us now.

If we have entered into the divine union we shall bear the divine fruits of a Christlike life and conversation. Pay no regard to your feelings, but see to it you have the vital fruits of a oneness in character and walk and mind. Undeveloped Christians often have powerful emotional experiences. I know one who was often kept awake by sweeping "waves of salvation," as she expressed it, yet she was far from honest in her dealings with others. No one could possibly believe she knew anything about a real divine union, in spite of all her fervent emotions.

It is as though Christ were living shut up in a far-off closet, unknown and unnoticed by the dwellers in the house, longing to be one with them in their daily lives, but unwilling to force Himself upon their notice, because nothing but voluntary companionship could meet or satisfy the needs of His love. Lonely days and weeks pass by for Him; they remain in ignorance, with no thought of the wonderful Guest.

Suddenly, the announcement is made, "The Lord is in the house!" Will its owner call out an eager thanksgiving and throw every door wide; or hesitate, afraid of His presence, seeking to reserve some private corner for a refuge from His all-seeing eye?

Far more glorious than having Christ a dweller in house or heart is to be brought into union with Him and be one—in will, purpose, interest, life. Words cannot express such glory. It seems too wonderful to be true that we are created and commanded to enter into this life. The Lord will not force it on us. The bride must say a willing "Yes" to the bridegroom, or the joy of their union is wanting.

The steps are but three: be convinced the Scriptures teach it; surrender our whole selves; believe He has taken possession. We must let doing the Christlike thing become, by constant repetition, the attitude of our whole being. We must begin to reckon ourselves dead and to reckon Christ as our only life. As surely as we do, we shall come to understand what it means to be made one with Christ, as He and the Father are one. Christ left all to be joined to us; shall we not also leave all to be joined to Him?

CHAPTER 19
THE CHARIOTS OF GOD

It has been said, "earthly cares are a heavenly discipline." They are even better—they are God's chariots, sent to take souls to high places of triumph.

They do not look like chariots, but like enemies, sufferings, trials, defeats, misunderstandings, disappointments, unkindnesses. Could we see them as they really are, we should recognize them as chariots of triumph in which we may ride to those very heights of victory for which our souls have been longing and praying.

The chariots of God are invisible. The king of Syria came up against the man of God with horses and chariots that could be seen by every eye, but God had chariots that could be seen by none save the eye of faith. The servant of the prophet cried, as so many have done since, "Alas, my Master! How shall we do?" But the prophet sat calmly within his house without fear. His eyes were opened to see the invisible; and all he asked for his servant was, "Lord, I pray thee open his eyes that he may see."

This is the prayer we need to pray for ourselves and for one another, for God's chariots are around us, waiting to carry us to places of glorious victory.

Whenever we mount into God's chariots, the same thing happens to us spiritually that happened to Elijah. We shall have a translation, not into heaven, as Elijah did, but into the heaven within us. We shall be carried from the low, earthly, groveling plane of life, where everything hurts and is unhappy, up into the "heavenly places in Christ Jesus." These places are interior, and the road that leads to them is interior, but the chariot is generally some outward loss or trial that afterward "yieldeth the peaceable fruits of righteousness."

In Solomon's Songs, we are told of "chariots paved with love." We cannot always see the love-lining to our own particular chariot; it often looks unlovely: a cross-grained relative or friend, human malice or cruelty or neglect. Look upon your most grievous chastenings as God's chariots sent to carry your souls into the "high places," and you will find they are indeed "paved with love."

The Bible tells us when God went forth, He "did ride upon His horses and chariots of salvation." It is the same now. The clouds and storms that darken our skies are really only God's chariots.

Have you made the clouds your chariots? Are you "riding prosperously" with God on top of them all?

A lady at a crowded convention was assigned a room with two women who wanted to talk when she wanted to sleep. The first night she lay fretting and fuming, long after the others hushed and she might have slept. The next day she heard about God's chariots. At night, she kept in undisturbed calm until very late then ventured to say slyly, "Friends, I am lying here riding a chariot!" The effect was instantaneous; perfect quiet reigned. If we would ride in God's chariots, instead of our own, we should find victory inwardly and outwardly, as she did.

We face constant temptation to trust in the "chariots of Egypt"—earthly resources. God is often obliged to destroy our earthly chariots before He can bring us to mount His, such as separating us from a dear friend or a minister on whom we lean too much to help us onward in our spiritual life. We have to reach the place where all other refuges fail us before we can say, "He only," instead of adding "He *and*—something else." Let us be thankful for every trial that compels us to take refuge in the "God that rideth upon the heavens."

Joseph had a revelation of his future triumphs and reigning, but the chariots that carried him there looked more like dreadful juggernaut cars of failure and defeat. Slavery and imprisonment are strange chariots to take one to a kingdom, and yet by no other way could Joseph have reached his exaltation. Our exaltation to the spiritual throne awaiting us is often reached by similar chariots.

The great point is to recognize "chariots of God" in everything that comes to us, and to learn how to mount into these chariots. He may not command or originate the thing, but the moment we put it into His hands, it becomes His. He at once makes even bad things work together for good to all who trust Him. All He needs is to have it entirely committed to Him.

Take each thing wrong in your lives as God's chariot, no matter if the builder of the wrong be men or devils. The enemy may try to turn it into a juggernaut by taunting that God is not in it. Overcome such with confident faith. "God is my refuge and strength, a very present help in time of trouble."

You must not be half-hearted but wholly accepting. The soul that rides with God has views and sights the soul groveling on earth can never have.

A Christian woman told me, "I am poor and have grieved I could not drive in a fine carriage. Now I know my life is so filled with chariots, I shall never need to walk again." There is no need for anyone to walk for lack of chariots: That misunderstanding, that mortification, that unkindness, that disappointment, that loss, that defeat—all are chariots waiting to carry you to the very heights of victory you have longed to reach. Mount into them with thankful hearts, and He will "carry you in His arms."

CHAPTER 20
THE LIFE ON WINGS

One aspect of this life hid with Christ in God has been a great help and inspiration to me and may be also to some other longing and hungry souls. It is what I call the life on wings.

This "cry for wings" is as old as humanity. Our souls were made to "mount up with wings" and can never be satisfied with anything short of flying. Like the captive-born eagle that feels the instinct of flight and chafes and frets at its imprisonment, hardly knowing what it longs for, so do our souls cry out for freedom. We can never rest on earth and long to "fly away" from all that so holds and hampers and imprisons us here.

We try to escape by running east or west, north or south, ignorantly thinking to get away from trouble and often discover we have run from a "lion" only to meet a "bear" or be bitten by a "serpent" in our place of supposed safety.

We might name our wings Surrender and Trust. By these, we are carried into a spiritual plane of the "life hid with Christ in God," a life utterly independent of circumstances, that no cage can imprison and no shackles bind.

Things look very different to the caterpillar, creeping along the ground, once its wings are developed and it soars in the air as a butterfly. Similarly, the crawling soul that has "mounted up with wings" will see things in a new way.

I once spent three long winter months in London, during which we saw no genuine sunshine, because of the dense clouds of smoke that hung over the city like a pall. But I have seen that above the smoke, the sun was shining. Once or twice through a rift, I glimpsed a bird sailing above the fog in the clear blue of the sunlit sky. Not all the brushes in London could sweep away the fog; but could we only mount high enough, we should reach a region above it all.

To overcome means to "come over," not be crushed under; and the soul on wings flies over the world and the things of it. They lose their power to hold or bind the spirit that is made in very truth "more than conqueror."

Birds overcome the lower law of gravitation by the higher law of flight; the soul on wings overcomes the lower law of sin and misery and bondage by the higher law of spiritual flying, the "law of the spirit of life in Christ Jesus."

Why do not all Christians always triumph? They do not "mount up with wings" but live on the same low level with their circumstances, powerless against trials and sorrows, overcome by and crushed under them.

A friend once told me the difference between three of her friends. She said if all three should come to a spiritual mountain, the first would tunnel through it with hard and wearisome labor; the second would meander around it, hardly knowing where she was going, yet because her aim was right, she would get around it at last; the third would just flap her wings and fly right over it. If any of us have tried to tunnel through or meander around mountains in our way, we must rise into the clear atmosphere of God's presence, where it will be easy to overcome.

The largest wings cannot lift a bird one inch upward unless they are used. We must use the wings we already have: Surrender and Trust, or they will avail us nothing. From high places we shall see things through the eye of Christ that change our lives! Instead of stirring up strife and bitterness, we will escape by simply spreading our wings and mounting up to where our eyes see all things covered with a mantle of Christian love and pity.

The mother eagle teaches her little ones to fly by making their nest so uncomfortable they are forced to leave and commit themselves to the unknown world of air outside. God stirs up our comfortable nests and pushes us over the edge, forcing us to use our wings to save ourselves from fatal falling.

Only by use can wings grow strong, large and fit for the highest flying. A lady whose life was one long strain from a cruel, wicked, drunken husband was driven to use her wings and fly to God. During years of trial, her wings grew so strong from constant flying, when the trials were at their hardest, she felt her soul was carried over them on a beautiful rainbow and found itself in a peaceful resting place on the other side.

If either Surrender or Trust are wounded, we cannot fly. No earthly bars can imprison the soul, only barriers between us and the Lord from doubt or some indulged sin. The Lord warned of this danger in the story of those so burdened by earthly cares they could not come to the great supper.

The flying I mean is *principle*. Although joyous emotion may accompany, flying does not depend on it, just on entire surrender and absolute trust. A great deal of emotional flying is like a feather driven upward by a strong puff of wind, then fluttering down when the wind ceases.

The promise is sure: "They that wait upon the Lord SHALL mount up with wings as eagles." Not "may perhaps mount up" but "SHALL." May we each prove it for ourselves.